ABDO Publishing Company

BUGS!
Walking Sticks

Kristin Petrie

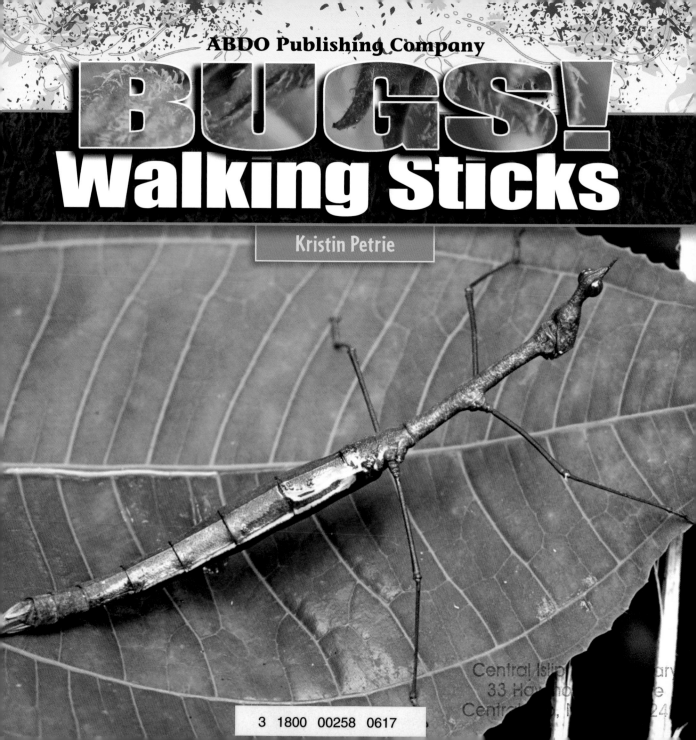

visit us at
www.abdopublishing.com

Published by ABDO Publishing Company, 8000 West 78th Street, Edina, Minnesota 55439.

Printed in the United States.

Cover Photo: Peter Arnold
Interior Photos: Andy Williams/CritterZone.com p. 7; AP Images pp. 12, 29; Corbis pp. 5, 21;
    Dennis Sheridan/CritterZone.com pp. 17, 18, 20, 25; iStockphoto pp. 19, 28; Jim
    Brandenburg/Minden Pictures p. 22; Joe Fuhrman/CritterZone.com p. 27; Mark Plonsky p. 11;
    Pete Oxford/Minden Pictures p. 23; Peter Arnold pp. 1, 8–9, 15, 19; Piotr Naskrecki/Minden
    Pictures p. 13; William Vann/edupic.net p. 18; USDA Forest Service/Bugwood.org p. 24

Series Coordinator: BreAnn Rumsch
Editors: Megan M. Gunderson, BreAnn Rumsch
Art Direction & Cover Design: Neil Klinepier

Library of Congress Cataloging-in-Publication Data

Petrie, Kristin, 1970-
  Walking sticks / Kristin Petrie.
     p. cm. -- (Bugs!)
  Includes index.
  ISBN 978-1-60453-073-5
  1. Stick insects--Juvenile literature. I. Title.

  QL509.5.P48 2009
  595.7'29--dc22
                              2008005929

Contents

Wacky Walking Sticks

You've seen leaves and twigs moving in the breeze. But have you ever seen a stick walking away? Wait a minute, sticks don't walk! In fact, that stick isn't a plant at all. It is a cool bug called a walking stick!

Walking sticks look just like the plants they live on. These insects are very well disguised. They seem to appear and disappear right before your eyes.

In reality, these bugs don't disappear. They simply blend into their **environment**. Walking sticks come in many shapes, sizes, and colors. Each one blends perfectly into its own surroundings. No other insect can compete with this camouflage!

Most walking sticks have skinny, twiglike bodies. These tricky creatures even position themselves in ways that resemble the branches on which they rest. Keep reading! You will learn fascinating facts about the sticks and twigs that can walk.

*A walking stick's body color may help it
blend in with tree branches.*

What Are They?

Like all insects, walking sticks belong to the class Insecta. Walking sticks are also from the order Phasmida. **Entomologists** are working to determine the number of families in this order. Many believe there are four families.

Stick-shaped insects, or walking sticks, belong to the family Phasmatidae. In Greek, *phasma* means "ghost." This is the perfect description for these disappearing stick insects! The entire order Phasmida has about 2,500 species. Of these, about 2,000 species are walking sticks.

Each species of walking stick has a two-word name called a binomial. A binomial combines the genus with a descriptive name, or epithet. For example, a two-striped walking stick's binomial is *Anisomorpha buprestoides*.

BUG BYTES

One of the longest known insect species is Acrophylla titan. *This walking stick can grow more than ten inches (25 cm) long!*

Some phasmid species are known as walking leaves. These insects have wide, flat bodies that look like leaves.

THAT'S CLASSIFIED!

SCIENTISTS USE A METHOD CALLED SCIENTIFIC CLASSIFICATION TO SORT THE WORLD'S LIVING ORGANISMS INTO GROUPS. EIGHT GROUPS MAKE UP THE BASIC CLASSIFICATION SYSTEM. IN DESCENDING ORDER, THEY ARE DOMAIN, KINGDOM, PHYLUM, CLASS, ORDER, FAMILY, GENUS, AND SPECIES.

THE PHRASE "DEAR KING PHILIP, COME OUT FOR GOODNESS' SAKE!" MAY HELP YOU REMEMBER THIS ORDER. THE FIRST LETTER OF EACH WORD IS A CLUE FOR EACH GROUP.

DOMAIN IS THE MOST BASIC GROUP. SPECIES IS THE MOST SPECIFIC GROUP. MEMBERS OF A SPECIES SHARE COMMON CHARACTERISTICS. YET, THEY ARE DIFFERENT FROM ALL OTHER LIVING THINGS IN AT LEAST ONE WAY.

Body Parts

Like all insects, walking sticks have three body **segments**. These are the head, the thorax, and the abdomen. Walking sticks also have two antennae, six legs, and an exoskeleton.

The walking stick's exoskeleton has several jobs. It gives the insect its body shape, and it protects the insect's **organs**. The exoskeleton also helps the walking stick blend into a plant or a tree.

For example, a walking stick with a prickly exoskeleton can blend into a prickly plant. And, a walking stick with a rough, barklike **texture** could be hiding on a tree!

However, the best camouflage may be the walking stick's color. Walking sticks range in color from bright green to dirty brown. Some walking sticks are many colors, while others are one solid color. Again, this depends on the walking stick's **environment**.

LEG

BUG BYTES

Some walking sticks change color due to changes in temperature or light. For example, walking sticks may become darker at night or on cool days. This helps them absorb extra heat.

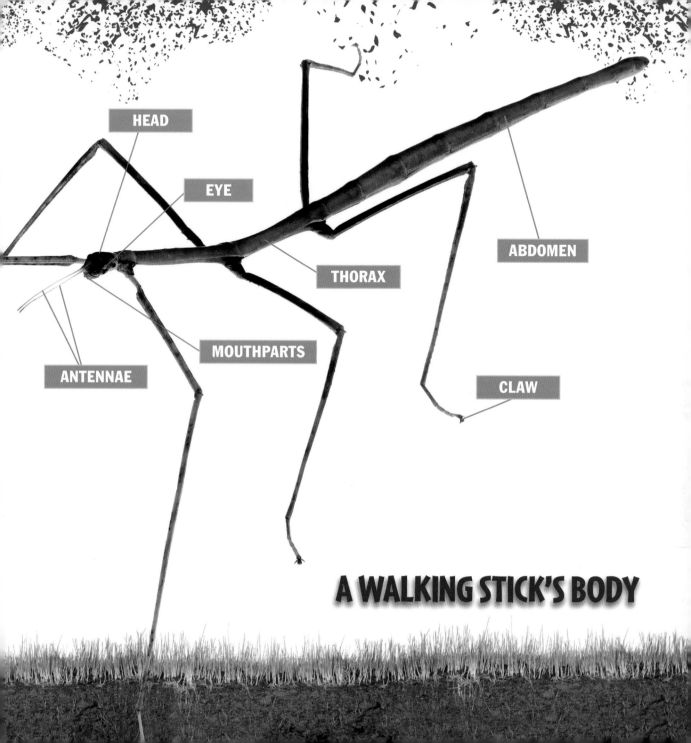

HEAD

EYE

ABDOMEN

THORAX

MOUTHPARTS

ANTENNAE

CLAW

A WALKING STICK'S BODY

A walking stick's first body **segment** is its head. The head may be long and flat or short and round. Whatever its shape, the head has several important features.

First, two compound eyes give the walking stick great vision. Compound eyes are made up of many lenses working together as one. In addition, some walking sticks have simple eyes called ocelli. These eyes detect light and dark.

The head also features two antennae. Antennae are an insect's communication and navigation tools. For example, antennae help the walking stick sense its surroundings. The walking stick also uses its antennae to receive **pheromones**. These chemical messages help the walking stick find food, sense danger, and more.

The walking stick's mouthparts are at the front of the head. Two sets of feelerlike palpi stick out in front of the bug's jaws. These palpi help the walking stick find a yummy treat. Then, the jaws get to work.

A walking stick has two sets of jaws. The first set, called mandibles, are strong and sharp! Mandibles are needed for tearing apart tough plant fibers. The second set, called maxillae, help chew the bug's meal.

The head is the walking stick's smallest body segment. Many of these bugs have small, rounded heads that can resemble the end of a stick. This shape may help disguise them from predators.

Behind the walking stick's head is its thorax. The walking stick's six legs all connect to this body **segment**. These long, jointed legs are pretty cool. Each leg ends in a sharp claw and a sticky pad. These features help the walking stick hold on to its perch. It can easily hang upside down or sway in the wind.

A giant walking stick

The walking stick's skinny legs are fragile. They may break and even fall off. Luckily, this is not a problem for young walking sticks. If the insect has not yet reached adulthood, it can grow a new leg! This process is called regeneration. However, adult walking sticks are out of luck. They cannot regrow a lost leg.

Some tropical walking sticks have two sets of wings attached to their thorax. The hind wings are thin and delicate. These wings are used for flight. The outer set of wings has a shell-like coat. These forewings fit over the hind wings when not in flight. They form a protective covering over the base of the hind wings.

The abdomen is the third and final section of the walking stick's body. This long **segment** houses many of the walking stick's **organs** and body systems.

Many walking stick species are wingless. Yet some species have large, colorful wings. These may be used for flight or to startle predators.

The Inside Story

A walking stick's body is long and skinny like a twig. Yet, it has room for all the **organs** and systems the walking stick needs to keep its body moving.

The walking stick has an open circulatory system. This means blood flows freely through its body. Walking stick blood is called hemolymph. The bug's long, tube-shaped heart pumps hemolymph from one end of its body to the other.

Spiracles and tracheae make up the walking stick's respiratory system. The spiracles are holes found along the sides of the exoskeleton. Air enters the spiracles, which connect to the tracheae. Tracheae are tubes that run throughout the walking stick's body. They deliver oxygen to all of its body parts.

The walking stick's **digestive** system has three parts. The first part is called the foregut. This is where food enters the walking stick's body. The foregut leads to the midgut. There, food is digested and absorbed. Following the midgut is the hindgut. Waste is released from this last section.

Hemolymph is much different from human blood. Our blood carries oxygen and is red. A walking stick's hemolymph does not carry oxygen. And, it is a greenish yellow color!

Transformation

A walking stick's life cycle has three stages of development. These are egg, nymph, and adult. The walking stick undergoes an amazing transformation from one stage to the next. This process is called incomplete **metamorphosis**.

For most species, the life cycle begins when a male and female walking stick mate. This long process takes hours or even days to complete. **Entomologists** are unsure of the reason for this long mating period. Perhaps the male hangs around to prevent additional mating.

After mating, female walking sticks have several ways to lay their **fertilized** eggs. Some species simply drop their eggs one at a time as they move about. Other species bury their eggs. Still others glue their eggs under leaves and on trees. These eggs may be arranged individually or in interesting patterns.

BUG BYTES

Depending on her species, a female stick insect may produce from 100 to 1,300 eggs.

Male walking sticks are much smaller than females. This makes it easy for females to carry males during long mating periods.

Some walking sticks lay their eggs with a quick twist of the abdomen. These species fling their eggs up to 20 feet (6 m) away! What kind of mother would send her eggs flying? Actually, this is a great way to keep the eggs safe.

Predators locate their walking stick prey by scent. A walking stick mother that throws her eggs does this to spread them out. This makes it difficult for predators to find many of the eggs. So, the mother increases the chances that her eggs will survive.

The walking stick egg itself provides additional protection. Each egg has a strong shell. It protects the young insect from extreme

LIFE CYCLE OF A WALKING STICK

EGG

NYMPH

temperatures. Also, the egg is colored and shaped like a seed. So many predators overlook it.

The length of the egg stage depends on the species. Some walking stick eggs hatch after just three months. Others remain in the egg stage for more than one year. Most stick insects hatch from their eggs during the spring months.

ADULT

When an egg hatches, a baby phasmid emerges. This tiny version of its parent is called a nymph. The nymphal stage of development is filled with growth.

In fact, nymphs grow so fast they burst right out of their skin! Luckily, a larger exoskeleton waits below. This process is called molting. Walking sticks molt five to six times during the nymphal stage.

When growth is complete, the walking stick enters the adult stage. Adult walking sticks are between 2 and 12 inches (5 and 30 cm) long. The largest walking stick species are the world's longest insects.

Some adults immediately begin searching for a mate. Interestingly, other walking stick species don't need males to complete their life cycle! Females of these species can produce eggs that do not require **fertilization**. Their eggs develop into more female walking sticks. Therefore, males of these species are not commonly found.

A newly hatched walking stick may stretch out to more than one-quarter of an inch (.6 cm) at birth.

Most stick insect species that produce unfertilized eggs can only create females. Yet, the species Ctenomorphodes tessulatus can also produce males in this way.

After molting, most walking sticks eat their old skin. This makes a healthy meal. It also prevents predators from discovering their location.

Plant Homes

Walking sticks are found in many places around the world. The cooler, northern regions of the world are home to several species. For example, North America and Europe have around 40 walking stick species.

However, most insects from the order Phasmida stick to warmer climates. The greatest number of stick insects in the world live in Australia and

Some giant walking sticks like to hide among tall prairie grasses.

Southeast Asia. Africa and Central and South America also have many phasmid species.

Walking sticks love warm, tropical places. The reason for this is obvious. Walking sticks live in, sleep on, and eat plants. Every inch of rain forest provides protection, a nice bed to sleep on, and food to eat. Wooded areas and grasslands offer these same comforts.

Many tropical walking stick species are larger than North American species. One example is the Australian giant prickly stick insect. This insect has a large, heavy abdomen.

Favorite Foods

By now, you know that walking sticks eat plants. In fact, all phasmids are herbivores. This means they eat only plant material. They do not eat insects or other creatures.

Some walking sticks may become pests if their populations grow too large. For example, the species Diapheromera femorata *munches on oak tree leaves. Too many of these insects can destroy the trees.*

Some of the walking stick's favorite plants are very prickly. These include the leaves of rose, raspberry, and blackberry bushes. Other favorites include many types of grasses and tree leaves.

Most walking stick species feed on a single type of plant. Others pick from a small number of plant types. Interestingly, walking sticks do not always

The Australian giant prickly stick insect is also known as the Macleay's Spectre stick insect. This species enjoys a wide variety of Australian plants in its diet.

eat the plant on which they rest. These walking sticks pick separate plants for day and night.

Walking sticks are **nocturnal**. At night, these critters are ready to start their day. What do walking sticks like to do first? They like to eat! Some phasmids dig right into their leafy meal. Others must move to their feeding spot to eat. By dawn, they are ready to rest again for many hours.

Beware!

With so many predators out there, walking sticks need protection. Being invisible is their best method of defense. Their body shape and color make this pretty easy. Yet if they are spotted, walking sticks are also experts at playing dead.

Walking sticks use more than their appearance to blend into their **environment**. These insects even move like sticks and twigs! Walking sticks take slow, careful steps. With each stride, they rock back and forth. This style of movement imitates the way branches move.

If all else fails, some walking sticks use other defenses. Being **nocturnal** helps walking sticks avoid enemies. Spiders, lizards, snakes, birds, and rodents all love to feast on stick insects. Many of these enemies are less likely to see their phasmid prey in the dark.

BUG BYTES

Walking sticks can precisely aim their toxic spray up to 16 inches (40 cm) away!

Larger walking stick species may have **spines** on their legs. These are used against predators. They also defend against competing males when mating.

Other walking sticks **secrete** a toxic liquid from joints in their exoskeleton. This poison spray can burn a human's eyes and skin. It also tastes bad to other animal predators.

Not all walking sticks match their surroundings. Some walking sticks eat toxic plants, which turn them bright colors. Their bright coloring warns predators to stay away.

Walking Sticks and You

In general, walking sticks are harmless. In fact, some species have become popular pets. These insects need only food, water, and a leafy place to live. This makes them easy to care for.

Phasmids remain mysterious creatures. **Entomologists** have many questions about how these insects live. Their population in the world is not yet known. For example, the Lord Howe Island giant stick insect was once considered extinct. Amazingly, it has reappeared in parts of Australia!

On the other hand, walking sticks can become too numerous. In these cases, entire fields and wooded areas are stripped of their grasses and leaves.

Sighting a walking stick is rare. Depending on where you live, you may never see one. However, look very carefully in gardens or grassy areas. If you are lucky, you may spot one of these ghostly insects!

Some stick insects, such as the Indian walking stick, are safe to observe up close.
Just remember to be gentle if you are lucky enough to hold one!

Glossary

digest - to break down food into substances small enough for the body to absorb. The process of digesting food is carried out by the digestive system.

entomologist - a scientist who studies insects.

environment - all the surroundings that affect the growth and well-being of a living thing.

fertilize - to make fertile. Something that is fertile is capable of growing or developing.

metamorphosis - the process of change in the form and habits of some animals during development from an immature stage to an adult stage.

nocturnal - active at night.

organ - a part of an animal or a plant that is composed of several kinds of tissues and that performs a specific function. The heart, liver, gallbladder, and intestines are organs of an animal.

pheromone - a chemical substance produced by an animal. It serves as a signal to other individuals of the same species to engage in some kind of behavior.

secrete - to form and give off.

segment - any of the parts into which a thing is divided or naturally separates.

spine - a stiff, pointed projection on an animal.

texture - the structure, feel, and appearance of something.

How Do You Say That?

antennae - an-TEH-nee
camouflage - KA-muh-flahzh
entomologist - ehn-tuh-MAH-luh-jihst
hemolymph - HEE-muh-lihmf
maxillae - mak-SIH-lee
metamorphosis - meh-tuh-MAWR-fuh-suhs
nymph - NIHMF
ocelli - oh-SEH-leye
Phasmatidae - faz-MAT-uh-dee
Phasmida - FAZ-mihd-uh
pheromone - FEHR-uh-mohn
tracheae - TRAY-kee-ee

Web Sites

To learn more about walking sticks, visit ABDO Publishing Company on the World Wide Web at **www.abdopublishing.com**. Web sites about walking sticks are featured on our Book Links page. These links are routinely monitored and updated to provide the most current information available.

Index